Unlock Your Why

7 Keys To A Thriving Relationship With Money

By Heather Burgette

Dear Tiffany,
You girl have been instrumental
in moving me towards my
dreams. I love you lotsa!
♥ Heather B

Cover design by Nirosha

Copy editing by Leilani Squires

Formatting by www.bookclaw.com

FIRST EDITION

www.heatherburgette.com

This book is dedicated to everyone who always believed that I'd write a book one day. "One day" has finally come. Thank you for always cheering me on!

Acknowledgements

To my husband, Blake – I remember you asking me about my dreams on our second date. You were never one for shallow conversations. Eleven years later, my dream to publish a book came true. I thought you were crazy suggesting at the beginning of 2019 that maybe I write a book this year. But just two months later, I decided to go for it. You took over dinners, handled bathtimes, put up with a messy house, and took the kids to the Y – all so I could write this book. I love you immensely.

To my kids – Tobias, Samara, Truitt, & Yana – you are so young still and barely understand what mommy is doing. When you are older, I hope my example is proof that there is no excuse strong enough to keep you from pursuing your dreams. You go for them! Dreams aren't convenient or easy. They require hard work and sacrifice, but they are worth it. Give your God-given gifts to the world.

To my mom and dad – Melanee & Ken Neilson – how do I thank you for your sacrifices and support over the years? I am a blend of you both – Mom's strength and Dad's demeanor. Dad, I still miss you more than I can express. Losing you made me realize just how precious and fleeting this one life is. I couldn't wait one more day to write this book. Mom, you were the first in my life to see what I was really capable of. You've known all of these 38 years that many books were growing in me. Thank you for fostering my dreams!

To my siblings – Jenny, Katie, Julie, Tiffany, Preston, Mykayla, & Haley – I just stare at your names and am in awe of the gift each of you has been in my life. Your texts, your cheers, your hugs, your talks – each in your own way have carried me along. You inspire me to live out who Heather is, not just by talk, but action as well.

To my in-laws on both sides – Tim, Dan, Abby, Pam, Jere, Andrea, Kevin, Angie, Derek – I love that my family continues to only grow. I watch how you live life and how you love those around you. Thank you for your support.

To my friends – you are spread out all over the world and yet you feel so close. Your cheers, your love, your support, your feedback, your input, your questions – you have become my sister-friends over the years. I love you each so very much!

To my beta-reading team – Thank you for signing up, for giving of your time, for sharing your input when the book was a brand-new baby. You'll always have a special place in my heart.

To my editor, Leilani Squires – who knew that our college writing classes would always keep us connected over the years? You did an awesome job with my rough draft. You are excellent in your craft. Thank you for all of your guidance and support.

To my Heartland Church family – you guys are awesome! Oh the healing and growth I've known in your community these past years. You guys are precious to me.

Table of Contents

Day Zero

A Poem for You, the reader

Written by Heather Burgette

I see you.

I see the shame that weighs you down. You feel surrounded by darkness, groping for hope.

You are captive, tormented by your thoughts and emotions.

You strike yourself with your own chains of shoulda-coulda-woulda because you know what you should do. But you don't do it. Instead, you succumb to a pattern that is comfortable.

You want to blend in. You want to feel and look like everyone else. After all, they appear to be having fun and enjoying life.

Their car, their clothes, the camps they send their kids to, the yearly vacations to Florida.

Oh, and there's the beautiful home, the remodeled kitchen, the smiles across their Pottery Barn dining room table.

Oh what a crafted world we live in and it's been crafted by the craftiest of all.

Behind this beautiful life are the truth of tears, arguments, and a marriage on the rocks. Bills piling, desperate measures taken to manage the chaos.

Balance transfers. Overdrawn accounts. The payday loan. That one investment too good to be true.

Still smiling and holding it all together. Just as you are, here in the darkness wrapped in your chains.

It seems that the web is too tightly woven to ever be free of it. There's just no way, you believe.

But now you hear my voice. You hear the hope in my lilt. You hear the freedom I've found.

And because you have nothing left to lose, you decide that just maybe, perhaps, it isn't too late for you.

So you reach out to me, you reach out for hope. You reach for air.

Yes, this whole time you've been suffocating; you had forgotten you weren't breathing.

You reach and step toward the pull of freedom. You still can't see in the darkness but you feel guided so you keep stepping forward.

Is that light?

You step back into the darkness, pausing because you don't feel you deserve the light.

After all, you were the one who willingly walked into the darkness.

But the draw to breathe freely and to move without chains is too great.

You continue on, stumbling along the way.

The light is brighter and you aren't used to such light, such ease of movement.

You hear the last clink and realize the last chain has fallen off.

"I'm free! I'm free! I'm free!" you shout with tears and dance with abandon.

This is life. This is freedom. This is how you were meant to be.

Week 1

Day 1

It starts with you

Hello, friend! I've written this book for you.

For what it's worth, I think you're incredible. Incredible for daring to believe there's more to life. Incredible for daring to break the chains of debt and change your family's destiny. Incredible for hoping that, maybe this time, it'll stick and you'll keep your promises to yourself.

Let me say it again: I think you are incredible. You are brave. You are focused and determined. You are willing to do the hard work. Go read it again because this is true, and you need to believe it.

For every person who reads this book, my dream is that you will become informed, feel hopeful, and feel confident in your personal finances. This is why I've poured out my heart, wisdom, and experience.

Did you notice three of those goals have to do with feelings? Our relationship with money is emotional, and man, they are strong feelings! We will explore those feelings and where they came from.

This isn't going to be a book of money fluff. This book takes work and focus. You'll have to write out your memories, thoughts, and intentions. It's not easy but it's worth it.

You know it. I know it.

I can tell you want this. You are done doing finances like this. You are done ignoring your finances and hoping it'll work itself out.

This won't be easy because people closest to you, friends and family, will tell you you're nuts for trying and you're nuts for wanting more. But, as my fitness coach used to tell me, "If it were easy, then everyone would be doing it!"

So let's start by making a promise:

I, _____, know I can change. I can break these chains of debt. I can save for my purchases. I can manage my resources well. I'm done doing money the way "normal people" do it. I can save for the legacy I want to leave behind for my loved ones. I want better and I will do the work to make it happen.

As you do the work in this book, you will discover your relationship with money changes. You will find yourself feeling hopeful, informed, and more confident at the end of this book.

So, let's begin this adventure of restoring financial freedom to you, your family, and to your community.

You know it's time. It's time to stop wishing things were different. It's time to stop hoping for a change. It's time to make that change happen!

THINK ABOUT IT, WRITE ABOUT IT

Spend a few minutes writing out how you hope to be different at the end of this book. What do you want to let go of? What do you want to gain?

_____

_____

_____

_____

_____

_____

_____

_____

Day 2
Illusion of truth

Today, we're talking about the impact of what we heard, and felt, about money from the adults in our lives as we grew up.

People tell me, "But you don't understand, Heather. I am too burdened. I can't care for my family the way I really want to. That's how it's always been—we've always struggled with our finances."

Why? Why has it always been that way?

Do you look at others and think, "I wish that could be me. They must be special in some way that I'm not." Perhaps you think, "Look at them flaunting their money. They are too rich. They're greedy." Let's explore those thoughts. Where did they come from?

Did your parents argue about money? Did they say things like, "Do you think I'm made of money?" Did they say things like "There's always too much week at the end of the paycheck. We'll never have enough."

Perhaps they said those people were rich because they were greedy.

Or, did they get a tax refund and spend it on a fancy dinner, or a lavish vacation, when really the credit card bill needed to be paid, or an appliance needed to be replaced?

Guess what? All of those emotions and words around money took root in your mind as a kid. They made little pathways in your brain. And every time you thought about money, the words you heard became your thoughts.

Have you ever heard of the Illusion of Truth Effect?

"It basically proves that any statement we read, see, or speak regularly is seen as more valid than one we're exposed to only occasionally. Amazingly, it makes no difference whether the information is true or false. The only thing that matters is how often we're exposed to it. Research from the University of California at Santa Barbara clearly shows that a weak message repeated twice becomes more valid than a strong message heard only once."

As you became older and began to have your own money, your experiences with money were reinforced by what you already believed about money.

You looked for confirmation to what you believed subconsciously about money, and then it happened as you expected. Then, you would say, "See, I knew it. There is never enough. I will always struggle... just like my parents." And so you lived life as you decided it would be.

It's a harsh pill to swallow and one we don't like to admit. We want to believe that life happens to us and we are at its mercy.

Yes, some things do happen to us and we have absolutely no control. I've been there. But most of my life and your life is a compilation of our choices and our decisions.

You may be saying you don't want to be poor or to struggle, but that's just how it is no matter how much you wish it were different. Do you really want different? Being different, having a different life, takes action.

Are you ready for hope? The definition of hope is "a feeling of expectation and desire for a certain thing to happen."

I don't think we can feel hope until we have a plan.

> Hope comes from being able to see down the road and know our actions today are impacting tomorrow in a good way.

THINK ABOUT IT, WRITE ABOUT IT

List the positive and negative phrases and emotions about money the adults in your life used as you were growing up.

_____

_____

_____

_____

_____

_____

_____

_____

Day 3
Memories of money

Picture yourself, about the age of eight, sitting on the living room floor and watching TV. You hear voices in the dining room but you don't quite know what they're saying. You lean to see what's going on. You're a kid. You're curious.

Your parent is hunched over the table, head in hands, and papers spread out all over the table. You see shoulders shaking and you think maybe you hear crying. The other parent suddenly starts yelling about money and how there's never enough.

"Anytime we get a little ahead, we get knocked down. There's no hope!"

Now skip into the future three years. You walk by the dining room on your way outside to play. Again you see your parent sitting at the dining room table, crying again. Stressed again. Saying the same words you've heard over the years. You continue to see your parents struggle year after year. You tell yourself, "That will never be me. I'll make sure of it."

> The adults in our lives tell us the most formative stories about money without realizing how those stories will shape our own interactions with money.

If you are set on changing your mind about money, then start by remembering the money story you grew up believing. We did some reflection on this yesterday.

I remember my parents arguing about money. It wasn't always because of the lack of it—sometimes it was about getting the bills paid on time. Sometimes it was other things.

Overall, the emotions around money weren't all bad memories for me. I clearly remember my mom getting her cash for groceries and man, could she stretch those dollar bills! She was amazing at providing awesome dinners for our large family. It wasn't until I started public school in fifth grade that I noticed the difference in my clothing and shoes—I didn't have trendy anything. Sometimes I cared, and sometimes I didn't. But I sure as heck noticed!

In middle school, I began to tell myself we didn't have enough money to buy things that mattered. It wasn't the truth, but it's how I organized my world at that age. Any middle-schooler wants to fit in, not stand out.

Our relationship with money is powerful.

We learn how to earn money through work, perhaps we even learn how to save it and spend it. But are we shown how to have a healthy relationship with money? Probably not. Our relationship with money is powerful. Money can run everything in our lives if we don't have an intentionally healthy relationship with it.

We're going to start now and rebuild this relationship the way it was intended.

THINK ABOUT IT, WRITE ABOUT IT

What promises about money did you make to yourself as you grew up? How have these played out so far in your life?

_____

_____

_____

_____

_____

_____

_____

_____

_____

_____

Action Day

"Without action, the best intentions in the
world are nothing more than that: intentions."

— Jordan Belfort

Welcome to your first day of action. Sir Francis Bacon was once attributed as saying "Knowledge itself is power." I believe knowledge is only powerful when you act on it. If you truly want to see a change in your life, and in your finances, then take action with your knowledge. Too often we get caught up in our heads, believing we need to have it all figured out before we act. But having it figured out never comes, and we waste precious time while allowing our excuses to stop us from taking action.

On the Mini Money Habits found in the back of the book, you will find a list to choose from. Some are one-time actions, some are to do once a year, and others require weekly or monthly attention.

Step 1: Pick the one that most needs your attention right now.

Step 2: Go do it. You are stronger than you realize and more capable than you believe. (Remember that we're building new beliefs on this journey.)

Step 3: Take the next few days and act on what you chose to do. After you pick your one thing, write out below what you commit to doing.

I choose the _____ habit to act on, because

_____

_____

_____

_____

_____

_____

Week 2

Day 1

Borrowing $10,000

"Okay, miss, I see you are approved for a $10,000 personal loan with an interest rate of 34 percent. I'll send over the paperwork via fax today and then we'll transfer the money to your account immediately."

I breathed a sigh of relief. "That should help me pay off a couple of things and feel a little less pressure. I can handle the interest payment; it's only $325 a month."

Crazy? You're absolutely right!

The payment was only interest and so I should have realized I had no hope of ever making a dent in the principle. But I wasn't thinking at all. All I wanted was to feel relief while keeping my current lifestyle. Even after nearly two years of financial struggle, I hadn't woken up to what I was doing to myself, and to my future.

This was my lowest point. I couldn't see past the next day and I certainly wasn't going to tell anyone about my huge mess. As expected, I struggled to pay the minimum payment. And when I did pay it, I felt sick as I realized I wasn't touching the principle at all! When I decided to move back to Indiana from Los Angeles, I fell further behind.

Let's do the math here, friends: $325 per month x 30 months (I missed a few months, of course) = $9,750. Ugh! It makes me sick thinking I paid that much money in interest and late fees just to feel some relief. It wasn't like I was behind on rent or starving, or about to lose my car to the bank. But I couldn't handle the strain from paycheck to paycheck.

After it all was said and done, this $10,000 payday loan cost me more than double the original amount lent to me. The relief I hoped it would give me was barely momentary.

I would stare at my phone, heart pounding and palms sweaty. The collectors called every day, several times a day, for months. I couldn't answer. I didn't know what to say.

Better to not answer. Better to ignore it and pretend life is good. The truth? I was drowning. Nothing I did seemed to help.

How had I let it get this bad? It was just one little choice—a credit card. What was the harm? We often say this when dabbling in something we know we shouldn't and convince ourselves, "I'm fine. I've got it all under control."

I was in a pit—a deep, dark, dank pit of crushing debt. The worst part was knowing the only person I could blame was myself. Collectors hounded me daily. There were constant letters and even a visit to my place of work.

Late fees upon interest payments piled high. The persistent calls and letter notices from collectors haunted me throughout those three years. The time came for me to be completely honest with my fiancé about my situation. In order to make the best use of my money, we got a personal loan from our bank at a small interest rate. We took that loan and paid off the payday loan in full. This strategy can be the best one at times. It just depends on your situation.

So how did I end up in that mess to begin with? There are two key reasons:

1. I had no idea how to manage the income I had
2. I had no plan for my future

If I had stopped and worked on those two points, they would have impacted my life immensely.

What about you? Have you stopped to consider those in your own life?

THINK ABOUT IT, WRITE ABOUT IT

What was the biggest money mistake you made? How do you feel about it now? Why do you think you made that mistake? And what have you learned?

_____

_____

_____

_____

_____

_____

_____

_____

Day 2
I was the thief

I am a recovering thief. I didn't sneak a piece of candy at the local gas station. I didn't steal mascara from the pharmacy. It wasn't a cute tank top from the mall. No, what I stole was far worse.

While I have been released from this shame, I am still dealing with the consequences of my days of thievery. I served jail time for my actions.

Oh, not a physical jail, but a jail made of mental walls, an emotional floor, and bound by spiritual chains.

My days as a robber began when I moved out west for adventure and a change of scenery. Little by little, I got caught up in the lifestyle of robbing. It was thrilling, to say the least. I felt trendy, accepted, and noticed. I felt I owed myself this lifestyle and deserved to live well.

The life of robbery afforded me many favorite things:

Weekly visits to my favorite salon for that pedicure

Regular nights out with the girls to enjoy dinner at a cute bistro

Seeing the latest flick on the big screen whenever I wanted

Daily trips to Starbucks for my favorite drink

A new laptop

Browsing the mall for another cute top to wear, a purse to carry, or shoes to enjoy

After a year of this fast life, it stopped being fun. I started to feel a little paranoid that I'd get caught. Surely, I couldn't keep this up. But when I decided I wanted to get out, it was too late. I'd stolen too much. There wasn't a way out.

I began to face my actions, knowing I had to pay back what I had stolen. That was the only way to be free. However, it wasn't until several years later when I fully realized who I had robbed.

You see, the person I had robbed was me. By spending wildly instead of saving and spending wisely, I had robbed myself in big ways.

For me, the consequences hit like a ton of bricks once I got married. My days of robbery resulted in:

No exciting vacations with my husband

Delaying starting a family

No fun purchases to make our house a home

No extra social adventures like concerts

We had to pay off those debts if we wanted a different life for us and for our family.

The biggest reality I had to face was that I—me, Heather—had done that to myself. No one else had forced those robbing days on me. I had chosen to live that way.

My life of fast spending and no saving for those couple of years was holding up future me at gunpoint. "Hey, I'm robbing you! Give me your dreams and goals. I need to use them for money so I can have what I want now. I must have these things!"

I'm thankful that my thieving days are over. I'm glad the time has been served. Now, I think ahead about future Heather and what she might need.

THINK ABOUT IT, WRITE ABOUT IT

Have you ever robbed yourself? What did you lose as a result?

_____

_____

_____

_____

_____

_____

_____

_____

Day 3
Start with the end in mind

Do you have a plan, a vision for your future? Scripture says, "Where there is no vision, the people perish."

Here's what I've learned about VISION over the years:

Veritas

This means truth. Truth is key in my life. We even named our third child, Truitt which means truth. When we have a vision for our lives, truth is at the core of it.

We have the truth of Him who guides us. We use truth as the lens through which to understand circumstances, ourselves, and those around us so we have a solid foundation on which to build our lives.

Imagination

The vision of our lives is ever-evolving. As we move from point to point, we realize the joy of the journey lies in imagining what's next for us.

We each are creative beings. Whether it be painting, singing, playing, cooking, drawing, photographing, we all have at least one outlet through which we feel right and we know we're close to the Creator of everything.

Vision is a chance to imagine what the next step is and to be excited about the life we have before us!

Self-discipline

This is a powerful concept that depends on you and me. We make it happen. No one can do it for us. I didn't fully understand the power of self-discipline until my husband and I began paying off our debt. Those early years of not updating our home, or taking vacations before we had kids, not buying fun toys, taught me self-discipline is the traction that moved me from setting the goal to meeting the goal.

Self-discipline is what helped me to lose the baby weight (not one time, but four times) and run four half marathons. Self-discipline moved me from wishing I would write a book one day to being intentional with seeking out writing opportunities.

The apostle Paul, from his jail cell, excitedly writes to his friend Timothy in, "For God will never give you the spirit of fear, but the Holy Spirit who gives you mighty power, love, and self-control."

Read that again.

Now read it again out loud this time. Let it soak in.

As believers of Christ, we have access to all we need today.

Innate

This is simply what comes naturally to you. The vision for your life isn't to be forced or conjured up. But it does take time to listen to yourself. Perhaps for many years, you've been ignoring that inner voice. If you are determined to begin living your life on purpose, you must be aware of the gifts you have and how you were created to impact the world.

When you realize you love doing something, and determine to take one step each week toward learning or doing something more with that, it will bring change to your life instead of wishing for it for years.

Organization

Setting a vision for your life brings organization to your choices. It drowns out the distraction noises and clarifies this step leads to that step, which leads to the next one, and so on. Start by organizing and living on purpose.

New

Vision is hopeful and thrilling. It's the promise of something to come. It says, "This journey is going to take me to new places where I'll meet new people and try new things."

Let me remind you of the point of all of this: to cast a vision for your life!

Sure, life changes and brings many unexpected challenges. However what is never, ever taken away from us is our choice, no matter the situation. Today, you have a choice. In two years, do you want to look back and know you did the best you could with what you had? Or will you shake your head and think "What the heck happened? How did I get here? And I still don't know where I'm going."

I love how Brian Fourman puts it: "Planning for the future and worrying about the future are two separate things. Planning is very strategic. Worry can accompany it but it doesn't have to. Planning is rooted in actions and seeks to produce results that are thought out ahead of time. Because of that, there is less emotion involved. Worrying about the future is all about emotion. It's fueled by the unknown…by uncertainty."[7]

THINK ABOUT IT, WRITE ABOUT IT

Which of these VISION letters is the most challenging element for you? How could you overcome it?

_____

_____

_____

_____

_____

_____

_____

_____

_____

Action Day

"Action will destroy your procrastination."

— Og Mandino

Welcome to your next round of action days! I hope you are so proud of yourself for keeping with this journey. You have read and journaled some thoughts over the past few days. Now it's time to again take action on what you are learning.

Step 1: Pick a mini money habit.

Step 2: Go do it. You are stronger than you realize and more capable than you believe.

Step 3: Over the next few days, act on what you chose to do. After you pick your one thing, write below what you will do.

I choose the _____ habit to act on, because

_____

_____

_____

_____

_____

_____

_____

_____

_____

Week 3

Day 1

Is this a good trade?

> The mind is powerful. It impacts our actions and words.

It can convince us to stay in bed for just five more minutes of sleep. It can cause us to scream at the lady driving in front of us at the speed of molasses. The mind can rationalize why we don't have time or energy to do that workout we said we'd do. It can convince us to have all the tacos and margaritas because we deserve it—we worked hard this week.

The mind can keep us binging just one more episode of the latest Netflix release or scrolling our social media feed even though our body is shouting, "Hello! I want to sleep!"

The mind can brilliantly persuade us that browsing through Target is the best way to unwind after the day we've had. When we freak out as the cashier says "Your total is $105.98," your mind (in the voice of a yoga instructor) says, "It'll be alright. You needed that splurge. You deserved it." Hmmm… the mind sounds like a pretty awful friend, right?

So, how do we change it? It's easy to feel helpless and like a prisoner to our thoughts. Heck, our mind can even sway us to believe that this is just how we are, and we'll never overcome our obstacles. Well, you can change, and it all starts in your mind.

The other day, I saw a meme on Facebook about being helpless to control Target spending. Instead of laughing, I got miffed. Can't we expect more of ourselves? If you have the money, and you decide to spend it there, then wonderful! But most shopping isn't a decision or a plan. Your mind may have convinced you that you had a plan, but you didn't really. I'm exhausted from this culture conversation that we can let ourselves off the hook and not expect anything better. We can't face the difficult thing or we can't "adult today" because it's just too hard.

Okay, yes. It. Is. Hard. If you want to go with that flow, then you have to let go of something else. It's an exchange.

Are you ready for the trade? Okay, here it is:

In exchange for not doing the hard stuff now, you can have a lifetime of wishing and regrets.

For the easy now, you get to watch others live full lives. FYI spending all your dough at Target on a Friday night or Netflix binging is not a fulfilling life.

For the easy now, you get to work hard in your elderly years.

Y'all, I'm 37. It's not young. It's not old. But I'm finally understanding this powerful concept: I am in control of my mind. And you are, too.

You get to decide today

You get to decide that you'll get out of bed when the alarm goes off so you can start your morning right.

You get to decide to not let others' actions enrage you.

You get to decide that you'll do that workout, no matter what.

You get to decide just how many tacos you'll eat.

You get to decide to enjoy an episode of your favorite show and then let your body rest so it can thrive tomorrow.

You get to not walk into Target and use your money for that beach vacation instead.

Look at us! We're changing our thoughts so we can live this life to the fullest. It's a daily fight. Let's fight together.

THINK ABOUT IT, WRITE ABOUT IT

What is the best thing your mind ever convinced you to do? What is the most absurd thing your mind convinced you to do? What is one thought you'd like to stop having in your life and what can you replace it with?

_____

_____

_____

_____

_____

_____

_____

Day 2
Within your means

My favorite Starbucks drink used to be the iced caramel macchiato. While in graduate school, I got one nearly every morning. Even if I only purchased one macchiato three times a week, that comes to $702 a year. What? Now I wonder to myself, why wasn't I brewing coffee at home? I was struggling with money, big time. Yet I still had a weekly pedicure or manicure, went out to eat daily, loved going to the movies, buying new purses and shoes, and taking road trips to the mountains or the beach. I even signed up for a two-year gym membership on a credit card!

Let's not assume I was just an idiot with money. While my choices were idiotic, I did know how to steward my money. I'd been working since I was 12 years old. My very first job was detasseling corn. My first official part-time job was at the local Burger King. I learned how to save the money I earned, use it for stuff I wanted and even give to our church. Through college, I had two part-time jobs and managed my finances pretty well.

So what changed when I graduated? I moved to Los Angeles because I wanted a change of scenery. Living in a big city, the culture was very different. Eating out at the many cute eateries and international cuisines is a social event. It's how you spend time with people. I can count on one hand the number of times I was invited to a friend's home. When we spent time together, it was out doing things and going places.

Still, it was I who made the choice to spend money I didn't have on things I didn't need. For me, the heart of the matter was this: I am homesick. I am hurting. I am unknown.

I tried to cope with a lot of emotional issues by spending money. But I would have laughed in your face if you'd told me that's what was happening.

Some of you may be saying "Well, I'm doing the best I can, but I still can't make ends meet. I'm subsisting on Ramen noodles, playing board games with my friends, not taking trips. My paycheck barely covers my necessities of living."

Then let me ask you this: have you considered getting a second job or do you really need to be living where you're living? Re-evaluate where you are and why you are there. You may absolutely need to be where you are now. Then again, maybe not. All I'm asking is you be honest with yourself. Is there a different way?

It's not easy being honest, especially with yourself when what we thought we wanted so badly isn't working out. I had to decide I wasn't making life work in L.A. and that moving back to Indiana was the best choice for me.

The struggle to live within our means in any given season never ends. But it does get easier because your vision becomes clearer and your why becomes stronger—whether it's taking a trip to Europe, visiting family at Christmas, buying a car with cash, blessing a friend with groceries, or staying at home once you have kids.

The money will always be spent. We get to decide the best use of it. Isn't that powerful? We get to determine where our money goes. How totally awesome is that? We are in control of our money. Not the creditors, or the marketers, or our feelings.

> Our vision for our life determines how we use our money.

THINK ABOUT IT, WRITE ABOUT IT

What spending habits do you need to re-evaluate? Where would your money go if you were debt free and fully in control of every dollar?

_____

_____

_____

_____

_____

_____

_____

_____

Day 3
The "b" word

Why do we struggle with managing our money? Yesterday I shared how I struggled with spending habits. Now, it's your turn.

Which of these apply to you?
1. Don't know where your money has gone
2. Behind on priority bills
3. Withdrawing money at the ATM from your credit card
4. Not opening and reviewing statements
5. Maxed out on your credit cards
6. Scared to check your bank balance
7. Living in your overdraft
8. Only making minimum payments on credit cards
9. Your normal pattern is "see it, want it, buy it!"
10. Not shopping around for the best deals

Confession time: I lived life for three years doing the majority of that list. Even then, some of these I was forced to stop simply because I had no money left. Yes, in some cases, I had maxed out my cash advance.

My friends, there's hope. If you're looking at this list thinking, "Oh, I'm not that bad off. I just do two of those. I'm cool. I got it all under control." Don't be so sure. It's a slippery slope. Ask yourself, "Am I willing to pay the price?"

In the end, you pay much more than money. You pay with your dreams, hopes, relationships, confidence, and your ability to stand on your own two feet.

My issue was emotional, mostly. While I was lacking financial education, I was also using credit cards to buy fun—to fill the void in my life. It's not easy confronting these reasons, but it's important to face them. When you do, you increase your chance of setting new money habits and keeping them.

It took me years before I realized I had made a mess of my life was because I was trying to cope with a lot of junk. And I kept digging a deeper hole until I could barely see the light above me. The transition to getting out of that pit meant having incredibly difficult and vulnerable conversations with my fiancé as I faced the reality of my baggage.

What does it even mean to live within your means? Is it actually possible? Answers to this vary depending on your stage in life—whether fresh out of college, or starting married life, or on a steady, established career path.

Here are 10 tips from Mint.com[2]:
1. Know your income and expenses
2. Track your expenses
3. Separate needs and wants
4. Don't compete (with others' lifestyles)
5. Pay in cash
6. Keep an emergency fund
7. Save money wherever possible
8. Cut down on expenses
9. Boost your income
10. Don't deprive yourself

I absolutely love number 10. It gets to the emotion of our spending habits and how we use money.

My idea of keeping a budget used to mean that I couldn't have the things I enjoyed, like getting a pedicure. Not true! We can always find ways to still enjoy our lives.

Get creative. Maybe you don't give yourself $50 to $100 a week to go out to eat with your friends. Cut that down a little and then substitute a night out with a night in at someone's home where everyone brings food and still has a great time together.

Budget ≠ deprivation

Budget = freedom and control

A budget is where you are in control of your hard-earned money and you determine where it goes. Isn't that a much better feeling than being bewildered, wondering where it all went?

THINK ABOUT IT, WRITE ABOUT IT

What feelings or thoughts come to mind when you hear the word budget? Which one of the Mint.com tips would make the biggest impact on your finances if you began using it today?

_____

_____

_____

_____

_____

_____

_____

Action Day

"Nothing changes if nothing changes."
— Albert Einstein

Welcome to your next round of action days! Remember, if you truly want to see a change in your life and in your finances, then you need to take action with what you're learning.

Step 1: Pick a mini money habit.

Step 2: Go do it. You are stronger than you realize and more capable than you believe.

Step 3: Over the next three days, act on what you chose to do.

Then, write what you've picked and what you will do.

I choose the _____ habit to act
on, because

_____

_____

_____

_____

_____

_____

_____

_____

Week 4

Day 1
The lie we believe

There was a time in our culture when personal debt was extremely rare. If you needed something, you saved up and paid for it. Only in the last 100 years have we seen the gradual uptick in personal debt to the point that it's become a normal way of life.

Over the 20th century, Americans took on more and more debt. Credit cards allowed us to purchase everyday items with a short-term loan. The first credit cards came into use in the 1920s when companies like hotel chains issued them for use at their locations.

Check out these stats: In the 1950s, consumers' averaged debts of 31 percent of their income. By 2000, the average American had debt of 81 percent of their income. The average American now has about $38,000 in personal debt. Consumer debt reached $4 trillion by the end of 2018[3].

Those numbers are depressing and they just keep going! How did we get here? Why are we here?

> We are here because we bought a lie—hook, line, and sinker.

I call it "the layered lie" because we don't swallow it all at once. We hear it over and over as we slowly adopt this lie as part of our own belief system. Then one day, we look up and we see nothing but darkness. We can't do any of the things we really want to do because of the layered lie.

First, we start by believing we must have a credit card on hand in case of emergencies. Next, we pull out the credit card to cover a purchase we just couldn't pass up because it's a great deal. And we promise we'll pay off in a few months. In reality, it was an impulse purchase with no cash saved for it.

The next layer of this lie is that debt is actually good for us and we need it. After all, it is part of being a good consumer, or so we're told.

Lastly, we decide to believe that living life without debt is impossible. We look at what we owe and we decide to just live with debt. We decide this is how things will be. We decide that getting rid of the debt is just too impossible.

We pick up the pen, set it to the dotted line, and sign our name. In our haste, we miss the fine print below: "I agree to give away my power, choices, and my rights. I give up my dreams and ambitions. I give up what my family needs most for their future in exchange for enjoying the present of today."

How do you feel? Angry? Sad? Do you want to punch something? Do you feel overwhelmed? Hopeless?

That's why I'm here. I get it. Oh, do I get it. I, too, once believed the lie. But I decided to take action against the lie and climb out of my debt pit. And you know what? It's worth living debt-free; it's worth deciding to not believe the layered lie.

THINK ABOUT IT, WRITE ABOUT IT

What are your thoughts and feelings about "the layered lie"? What have you given up as a result of buying
into the lie?

_____

_____

_____

_____

_____

_____

_____

Day 2

Against the grain

I think one of the hardest things to do is to go against the grain—to swim upstream. Our culture is full of messages which amount to "Do what feels good now; screw the future!"

My husband and I decided to do the opposite. We decided to prepare for our future and swim upstream from the beginning of our marriage. Getting out of debt seemed like the smart choice and the wise way of setting up our life together.

At the time of writing this, we are celebrating 10 years of marriage and we have four incredible children. Like any family, we have our challenges. But debt is not one of them. We aren't stressed about payday or "what if…" scenarios. We still deal with emergencies. We get to decide how to use our money instead of it going out the door every month to creditors. Been there. Done that. Not going back.

We didn't get here willy-nilly. We did some of the hardest work during the first five years of our marriage. Gosh, those were hard years. It seemed like everything got thrown at us, including the tragic loss of my dad. Grief messes you up, and it can mess up a marriage as well. But we worked at it, learned, and grew.

Starting our marriage in debt and trying to pay it off as fast as possible was not easy. While we both were committed to the goal, we weren't on the same page as to how to get to that goal. We both knew it meant having our budget, living sparingly, and throwing all the extra cash we could at our debt. We both loved seeing the debt number go down, but we had started at a number of more than $75,000. Many of you are working with much bigger numbers. Some of you have much smaller numbers.

The journey to being debt-free is wrought with high highs and low lows but keep at it until you're free. Along the way, you must, must, must ignore our culture's messages about living for today and doing what feels good.

Be ironclad in your resolve to stay focused on your goals and achieving your freedom dream.

You've got this. You can do it. As you walk your path to freedom, others will be watching because, secretly, they're hoping that perhaps they can have freedom and peace in their finances.

So go on, show them it's possible. Show them, and yourself, that there is hope.

THINK ABOUT IT, WRITE ABOUT IT

What cultural money messages are most difficult for you to ignore? Has following them helped you in any way? What would change in your life if you chose a different way?

_____

_____

_____

_____

_____

_____

_____

_____

Day 3
Is normal good?

I'm a crier. I can cry easily at the smallest things. I think it's a family trait; we're absolutely okay with crying anywhere. Often I find myself crying when I see how people have overcome incredible odds. I cry when people show up in their life instead of just going through the motions. I cry when people stand up and say "Hey, world! This is who I am and what I can do!" Hahaha, I'm tearing up just writing those words.

Recently I cried watching a YouTube video of Katie Ledecky win a gold medal in the 2012 London Olympics. She was just 15-years-old and she had overcome the world stage. Can you imagine the hard work she put in? Imagine the sacrifices she made for early swim practice and after school practice. How many times did she have to miss out on the fun things her friends were doing? In saying yes to her dream of being an Olympic athlete, she had to say no to many other things that a normal teen-ager would do.

While we're not all destined to be a world-class ath-lete, I do believe we each are destined to live out the unique gifting inside each of us. We are destined to live in freedom.

> It's against our very nature to be chained up, to live life without choices or options.

Yet when we misuse our finances so we can fit in with everyone else, we lose our options to live life on our terms.

Believing the lie that debt is normal is the great money tragedy of the past 50 years. But believing that debt is normal is what has gotten us into this crazy finan-cial crisis in our country, the crisis that the majority of families are facing today. The personal finances of most Americans are dismal. The average savings of the Baby Boomer generation (ages 55-75) is $152,000[4]. If you combine that with the average Social Security check of $1,461 a month, then they're trying to live on $23,612 a year.

Let's look at a population of our culture who knows the burden of debt and the delay of their lives, thanks to debt. Millennials are delaying marriage, homeowner-ship, and starting a family. Not because they want to, but because they have such large student loans[5]. "Now, 44 million Americans are shouldering $1.5 trillion in outstanding student loans, with young people under the age of 35 holding almost half of that debt."[6]

I could go on and on and on with statistics, but you can see that we're in bad shape here, folks. Being normal has gotten us in a whole heap of trouble. Let's be differ-ent. Let's do this together. Let's change the tide of this country. Let's stop living for only for today and start thinking down the road, even a little bit. Let's think about the coming generations and the legacy we want to leave them.

THINK ABOUT IT, WRITE ABOUT IT

Which of these statistics surprised you? What would you want the next generation to say about how you used your money?

_____

_____

_____

_____

_____

_____

_____

_____

Action Day

"Only new actions will bring different results."
— Billy Cox

Welcome to your new set of action days! Are you starting to anticipate these yet? Remember, if you truly want to see change in your life and in your finances, then you need to take action with your knowledge.

Step 1: Pick a mini money habit.

Step 2: Go do it. You are stronger than you realize and more capable than you believe.

Step 3: Take the next three days and act on what you chose to do.

After you pick your one thing, then write out below what you will do.

I choose the _____ habit to act
on, because

_____

_____

_____

_____

_____

_____

_____

_____

Week 5

Day 1
The future you

We're so conditioned to buy when the sales happen because we have major FOMO (fear of missing out). We buy into the brilliant schemes of marketers so we run out to buy that couch that's 40% off for Memorial Day weekend. Do we *need* a couch? Most likely we do not.

> We are conditioned to buy, rather than to save.

At the moment, it's so easy to convince ourselves that we absolutely cannot pass up this deal or this want. And maybe you do need that car because the other one died. That's a need right there.

When I stop and look down the road at future Heather, and imagine what she'd want, then I am able to decide whether or not I really, really need this coffee, this camera, this couch, or this car. In my own journey, this is where the magic happened.

Perhaps you consider yourself a saver. That's awesome! What are you saving for? Is that money tagged for a purpose? If it isn't, then go decide what you are saving that money for. If you do not tag it, then one day it'll unintentionally be gone. Maybe you'll lend it to your adult kid who's gotten themselves into a financial emergency due to their own choices. If you do that, make sure you chose that instead of responding out of obligation or guilt. The point is to determine now what to use that money for.

I chat every day, online and in-person, with folks who are struggling with some aspect of their finances:

Budgeting is too hard

They overspend on their groceries by hundreds of dollars

They want to go on vacation with their kids but have no cash for it

They can't stop buying things

Saving for retirement is elusive and feels impossible

Inevitably the conversation turns to me asking about their future. "What about six months from now, or a year from now, or 10 years from now? What will you have wished you'd done now?"

It's a beautiful light bulb moment. And it's powerful. We see self-care help all over the place nowadays. But most people aren't doing it with their finances. A therapy trip to Target isn't self-care unless you are a magical person who can browse and buy maybe a couple of dollars items. Most of us can't. One money gal I follow on Instagram does not allow herself to get a cart at Target. She knows herself and so she helps herself by not browsing with a cart. What a great, tangible reminder of her intention to limit her spending there!

Recently my youngest sister graduated from college. Blake and I gave her a book on personal finances. What was most precious to give her was my wisdom, being 15 years ahead of her. I encouraged her to not do as I did and spend foolishly, without aim or vision. I challenged her to think of herself as a 32-year-old woman and consider what she might need at that point.

Perhaps she wants no debt. Perhaps she wants savings so she can buy her first home in cash. Perhaps she'll need a car. Perhaps she'll already have been investing a monthly amount into her 401k. Perhaps what she'll appreciate most is the peace of mind knowing her finances are in order.

What about you? What does the future you want?

THINK ABOUT IT, WRITE ABOUT IT

The future is vague and blurry. But I bet you can picture yourself in five or ten years. What do you want for that person? What is their day like? What is their financial situation?

_____

_____

_____

_____

_____

_____

_____

_____

Day 2
When motivation leaves

"So, we've crunched the numbers and our goal is to be debt-free in the next two to three years," we shared optimistically with family and friends. "But debt is a way of life," came the emphatic response from some.

We were newly married and had hit the ground running on killing our debt. In fact, we had talked so much about our financial situation before the wedding, that we knew what we needed to do before we said: "I do."

It was simple for us.
1. We wanted a family.
2. I wanted to be home with our kids.
3. We'd never be able to pay off the debt living on one income.
4. We didn't want a life of struggle, especially when it seemed within our control to live otherwise.

5. We decided to hold off on having kids and work as hard as we could to get out of debt.

Well, the plan didn't work as we originally hoped (nothing does, right?). Our original goal was to have it paid off in 2-3 years. But then...

1. Baby #1 was born. I went back to work part-time.
2. Baby #2 was born. I chose to stay home during the day and teach classes at night.
3. My online teaching assistant job was phased out.

However, we kept at it, determined to make this debt disappear. We kept motivated by little challenges between us, such as who could spend the least of their spending money to put towards a payment. We listened to Dave Ramsey's radio show, especially the "We're Debt Free!" calls. Those always had us crying at the end. We regularly talked with others about their own journeys.

It was an investment in our marriage because we learned how to discuss money, how to spend money, and how to work together to meet a goal. It was an investment in our kids because we wanted to provide cash-funded vacations. We wanted to provide them with a home where money was a tool and not a form of stress and unending arguments. We wanted to provide them with choices of what to do or not do, based on the best choice—not ever because we didn't have the money.

It was an investment in our future together because one day we'll be able to leave the jobs and we can spend our retirement giving generously, living with freedom, and pouring into ministries we love.

It was an investment in our legacy because, even after we're gone, those we love will benefit from this decision that two young people made to get out of debt and live differently.

Getting out of debt isn't just about not having debt.

It's about much, much more. It's about living life in freedom. It's about being able to have options instead of being stuck in a corner. Are you ready to invest in you, in your future?

THINK ABOUT IT, WRITE ABOUT IT

When you hear the term "financial freedom," what feelings or phrases come to mind? Do you think you're worth this investment of financial freedom? Can you think of any cons to being financially free? What is the biggest pro about being financially free that will help you accomplish your goal?

Day 3
The next generation

This week we've been talking about the future you and thinking about that person. Now let's shift to looking at the future generations coming. What do we want for them? What does *better* look like for them, in terms of their personal finances?

About a year ago, I was sitting in a living room with other moms. We were talking about our kids and our college experiences. Then the conversation turned to student loans and who had how many years left to pay. Of seven gals in the room, I was maybe one of two who had finished paying off those student loans. Keep in mind we all are almost 15 years out of college and most of the room still faced years of repayment.

One mom spoke up, "I loved my college experience and I definitely want my kids going to college. But they won't get any help from us. They can pay for their college just like we had to."

This grieved me. And I thought back to my parents. They provided well for our needs but could not save for our college funds. However, they helped me do everything possible to get scholarships and grants to help pay for college. Through incredible provision and my hard work, I earned an amazing four-year scholarship to a private college. It wasn't fully covered but I graduated in 2004 with less than $10k in student loans. That was pretty awesome. I wasn't tied down by my repayments but I also wasn't free.

I want even better for my kids, for this next generation. I don't want to see kids graduate (or not graduate) with thousands of dollars in student loans. They need better guidance from us adults. Let's give them a leg up instead of being okay with their struggle to pay back a massive student loan bill.

Go back to your own years as a young adult. How would your life be different now if you had been guided to grow into adulthood? What if you'd had a personal finance course, in high school and college and after graduation?

THINK ABOUT IT, WRITE ABOUT IT

Imagine your life without debt as a 22-year-old. What would it look like? Where would you have gone? What would you have done?

_____

_____

_____

_____

_____

_____

_____

_____

Action Day

"Vision without action is daydream. Action without vision is nightmare."

— Japanese proverb

Welcome to your next round of action days! You've accomplished so much over the past weeks.

Step 1: Pick a mini money habit.

Step 2: Go do it. You are stronger than you realize and more capable than you believe.

Step 3: Take the next three days and act on what you chose to do.

After you pick your one thing, write below what you will do.

I choose the _____ habit to act on, because

_____

_____

_____

_____

_____

_____

_____

_____

_____

Week 6

Day 1
It always comes back

Growing up, I watched my parents walk out a life of generosity. My dad was a handy guy and my mom was a thrifty but excellent cook.

It was normal for my mom to drop a meal off at a friend's house, to take a bag of groceries over to someone in need, to have people over to our home for dinner. My mom and dad did not let any excuse stand in their way of giving where there was a need. At least that was my viewpoint as a kid. Sometimes a need was running out to pick up a friend whose car had died. Sometimes it was raking leaves for a neighbor. Or sometimes the need was helping someone work on their home.

Their generosity kept their hands open and hearts willing to see the needs of those around them. As they gave to others, the generosity came back to them. My dad and mom raised eight children. For most of those years, my dad was a hard-working factory manager and my mom was home full-time with us kids. They didn't have a ton of money, but what they did have, they used with generous hearts.

This example of open giving impacted me. Their example drew me to a life of giving wherever I am, whenever I'm asked, however I can at the time. Over the years, I've been approached at a gas station by someone who needed gas money. I've dropped $10 in the hands of someone standing on a street corner holding a "need help" sign. I've given toys and clothes to a family who needed them. I've made dozens of meals for mamas with newborns, or friends stuck in their home, or someone recovering from surgery.

I've had enough experience to know that when I gave, I received something in return. One of the most generous returns to us has been a family member passing down all of her kids' clothes to my kids. Over the years, it has saved us hundreds of dollars. And she buys the cutest stuff!

One of my favorite give/receive stories is when I was headed to a friend's house with a meal. I needed to grab sour cream on my way. While standing in line to pay, I noticed a little girl and her dad in front of me. They were buying the basics, but his card wouldn't process the payment. I leaned forward and told the cashier that I'd pay for it. The guy was embarrassed but thankful that he could still get his groceries. And, I felt so thankful that I could help him out.

A week later, I was checking out at our local Aldi store. I always shop with cash so that I don't overspend. I had my two toddlers in tow and was pregnant with our third. And I had indeed overspent that trip because I had bought extra items for Thanksgiving dinner. The cashier pulled out a $20 bill and said, "I was given this to bless you today." My eyes filled with tears of gratitude. It was just $20, but it was so precious to me.

It's a universal law the Creator set in place so that we could experience the pure joy of giving and the blessing of receiving. When we give of our time, money, or other resources, they come back to us somehow.

THINK ABOUT IT, WRITE ABOUT IT

What do you remember about your parents being generous as you were growing up? Write about a time when someone blessed you with their time or money.

_____

_____

_____

_____

_____

_____

_____

Day 2

Inconvenient

Are you on the lookout for ways to bless those around you? Maybe it's the cashier at the store or the guy behind you at McDonald's. Maybe it's the family with young kids in the restaurant. Maybe paying a utility bill for a single parent in your community. Maybe it's cleaning the home of someone who has a loved one serving in the military overseas. Maybe it's that widow with three little kids.

I know a couple who sets aside their tax return every year and puts it into their generosity account. The money in this account is used throughout the year to help meet the needs they hear about. I love that concept. First of all, how wonderful to plan on being generous. It doesn't always have to be a spontaneous act, folks. And, they are intentionally looking for how they can give that money away to bless others.

Sometimes we are generous with our money, but not with our time. Or perhaps vice versa. We give of our time but we won't share our home or our table with those who need it most.

A family tradition we've started is to open our home for Easter dinner to friends at church, to those who may not celebrate that day with family. Our home is filled with the chatter of our friends interacting with our kids and the table is full of food. We eat and play games and enjoy each other. Over the years, I have gotten over the self-imposed expectation that my house has to look a certain way in order to have people over. I'm thankful for the examples in my life who've shown me hospitality isn't about the house, but about the welcome and warmth in that space.

Generosity doesn't look one specific way. But it does include all of us, used in different ways in different seasons. Yes, generosity is inconvenient or even sacrificial, but it is so worth that feeling of knowing you've blessed another person. Are you willing to discover how it'll always come back to you in beautiful, tender, unexpected ways? At the end of our lives, would we rather be thankful for all the ways we gave unreservedly, or would we rather regret how we were stingy with our resources?

THINK ABOUT IT, WRITE ABOUT IT

How do you feel when you get to give to others? If you could be outrageously generous with your money, what would you do?

_____

_____

_____

_____

_____

_____

_____

_____

Day 3
Too afraid

After more than five years of paying off our debts and another year building up our emergency savings, we were ready to begin investing 15 percent of our monthly income. During our monthly budget meeting, I stared at those numbers and could not get on board with my husband. After all, we had a growing family, and we were already putting aside money with his company's retirement account.

We talked it over and over for probably three to four months. I felt like this money could be used right now. Not only for our family, but also for generous giving beyond what we were already doing. To my husband's credit, he kept talking about it until I was ready to agree. One night he asked me, "Heather, don't you have dreams for our retirement years?" My eyes filled with tears as I realized my main issue. When I looked into the future, I saw nothing. I could not see our retirement years. I could not see him.

My dad passed away unexpectedly at the age of 53. This event impacted me greatly. What I didn't realize was that this traumatic loss had built an invisible wall to protect myself from those hopes and dreams in case, one day, I lost Blake and our later years together. You see, I wasn't only fighting trauma, but also a generational habit that was also a deep-seated fear. My dad had also lost his father at a young age. My dad hadn't saved much for his later years. I'm not sure, but perhaps he was fighting this generational fear.

I still have to work to see my own future. But it is slowly becoming clearer and brighter. Hope is returning. I began to dream with Blake about what might be my personal paths of generosity in our older years. Perhaps it's paying for a married couple to have a night out on the town while their kids are cared for. Maybe it's sending someone to clean house for a single mom. Perhaps it's providing the majority of funding for a family who is desperate to adopt a child. Maybe it's paying the tuition of a college student in our church.

Yes, I can contribute in small ways to these dreams today. But as we invest, our money grows. And then we make an even bigger impact in the Kingdom.

THINK ABOUT IT, WRITE ABOUT IT

What thoughts come to mind when you hear the word "investing"? Is it something your parents talked about or did during your childhood? If you aren't investing (growing) your money now, what is the obstacle to starting now and how can you overcome it?

_____

_____

_____

_____

_____

_____

_____

Action Day

"The most difficult thing is the decision to act; the rest is merely tenacity."
— Amelia Earhart

Welcome to your next round of action days! You've accomplished so much over the past weeks.

Step 1: Pick a mini money habit.

Step 2: Go do it. You are stronger than you realize and more capable than you believe.

Step 3: Take the next three days and act on what you chose to do. After you pick your one thing, write below what you will do.

I choose the _____ habit to act on, because

_____

_____

_____

_____

_____

_____

_____

_____

_____

Week 7

Day 1
Let's talk about it

You've probably heard that you shouldn't discuss money, politics, or sex. I think those are generally polite rules to follow. The problem with rules though is that when they get applied to all areas of life all of the time, then we're left feeling isolated with our big problem. We have no one to help us because "that's impolite to discuss."

About eight years into our marriage, my husband turned to me one night and said, "Honey, I think maybe we talk about money too much." I laughed. He wasn't wrong. We talk about our own money, and with other couples about their financial journeys, all the time. We are an open book about our own struggles and victories. We meet with couples who need direction on a decision or a plan of attack. Money is an open conversation for us. Talking about money is no longer foreign to me. At all. In fact, I am a self-proclaimed money nerd now.

Maybe it's that I really want others to know the hope and freedom I experience now.

One of the wonders of social media for me has been following and connecting with others who are on their debt-free journey. I have massive respect for them because I know how hard that journey is and how much dedication it takes. One day, a person shared how they feel as though they're leading a double life because no one in their personal life knows about their debt-free journey. Many others chimed in that they have separate social media accounts and also keep their journey a secret from friends and family.

I was stunned. I couldn't relate one bit. The first thing we did in our marriage was to share with family and friends what we were doing and why we were doing it. While some were skeptical of our ambitious goals, many were very supportive and cheered us along the way— all five years and three months of it.

On the other hand, I do understand why these folks keep it a secret. Often, our debt is what I term "stupid" debt. Out of desperation, or lack of knowledge, we mismanage our finances. That can feel embarrassing and shameful. We can even convince ourselves that no one else could understand our situation.

When I was in the throes of avoiding creditors' calls, delaying my student loan payments, and barely scraping by, I kept it all a secret. I felt completely alone. I felt ashamed. I felt as though I were the only person in the world who'd dug a hole this deep. I was certain I'd always be making up for these mistakes.

That loneliness was not motivating. At all. In fact, it only kept me in the desperation cycle of trying to figure it out on my own, continuing to make bad choices and hoping each one would be the ticket out of my mess. Yes, I'm shaking my head, wishing I'd just gotten into a personal finance class. I would have learned so much and saved myself thousands of dollars, not to mention I would have had people to walk alongside.

Four years into working to pay off our debt, I finally decided it was time to create a community for our journey. Yes, we had supportive family and friends but I wanted to make space for others who needed that help and inspiration as well. On October 22, 2013, I started a group on Facebook. Its name was "Becoming Debt Free" and the purpose stated:

The purpose of this group is to encourage, share, and inspire each other as we work towards being debt-free. Whether you owe $1,000 or $100,000, we encourage you *to share your struggles, your journey, and certainly your victories! Becoming debt-free can be a tough journey, long, and seemingly lonely. But we realize that others are walking next to us and we see that it's possible to indeed be debt-free, and it's just enough to help us over the next hurdle.*

Over the years, it's grown to more than 155 members. We're all heading in the direction of doing better with our finances. We understand that we are stronger together than apart. We know that each person brings fresh ideas to the table, whether cutting the grocery bill or negotiating an outstanding bill with a creditor. Finances, especially a hard situation, can feel so lonely.

What members are saying about this community:

"Just when I want to stop caring about budgets and getting rid of debt, someone posts a financial victory. Whether it's a big or a small victory, it is encouraging and suddenly spurs me on …. to finish the debt race!"

"It really helps with staying on track with your goals by being surrounded by like-minded people. I have also taken the opportunity to ask the group different questions regarding the level of interest we have, whether to give outside the tithe at church while paying off loans, etc… It's been a great resource!"

"It's a great place to get suggestions. And share victories—no matter how small, people always cheer for it and it helps keep the motivation up for other victories."

"When I want to just give it up, I come here and find one more reason not to."

You get the point.

> Community is a powerful and major key to financial freedom.

THINK ABOUT IT, WRITE ABOUT IT

Do you share about money struggles or victories with others? Why or why not? Have others shared their challenges with you? Where can you find community in your own financial journey?

_____

_____

_____

_____

_____

_____

_____

Day 2

In it together

No matter where we are in our money journey, we are more likely to succeed when we cheer on and remind each other why we're doing what we're doing. Thus, the Promise Posse was born. It's a local group of gals, of all ages and stages, who come together and take charge of their financial future 90 days at a time. Just 48 hours ago, the Promise Posse had our first local meeting. To say that it was beautiful is an understatement. Community and conversation can be powerful, and even necessary, especially when you're trying to live counter to popular habits.

Many ladies were interested in coming; six showed up. We started the meeting talking and learning and sharing, and sheer magic happened. We talked about the importance of keeping promises to ourselves and how we can stop breaking those promises.

We talked about how the commitment we make to our finances is no longer optional. We are done making excuses. We are ready to do the hard work. After each of us had picked at least one action item to focus on for the next 90 days, we read this promise aloud to the group:

I promise to me, _____, that by the date of Saturday, August 3, I will take the necessary steps to complete the task of_____. I will not allow my excuses to stop me. I will not let fear stop me. I will not listen to culture's messages about money. I will do this so that I can begin owning my financial future. I am valuable and I am worthy of keeping this promise to myself.

Now stop and read those words as if it were you making a promise to yourself. Imagine others hearing you say those words.

Powerful. Magical. There are many things I've experienced in community over the years. Heck, I grew up seven siblings! Perhaps being born into a community, into doing life with others, has always drawn me back to community—back to doing some part of my life with others.

Community with family

Community with college friends

Community with church family

Community with co-workers

Community with neighbors

Community with office mates

The definition of a community is "a feeling of fellowship with others, as a result of sharing common attitudes, interests, and goals."

I can look back at my life and see those dark spots. In addition to whatever was happening, I had also managed to cut myself off from the community because I was ashamed. At those times, I had myself convinced that no one else would understand.

One of my favorite authors, Brené Brown, says: "Shame corrodes the very part of us that believes we are capable of change."[8]

And that's the power of this community. We speak vulnerably, empathy comes back in response, and shame dissipates when we realize that many others are walking the same journey we are.

THINK ABOUT IT, WRITE ABOUT IT

Write about a time you felt shame about an area of your life. How did you handle it? Can you imagine telling others your secret?

_____

_____

_____

_____

_____

_____

_____

_____

Day 3
No longer hiding

Years ago, I read a news article that posed this question: "What if we all walked around with a physical sign of our debt amount? Would it challenge us to get rid of our debt or would it only further normalize debt?" That idea stuck with me. What if we couldn't hide the trouble we're in? What if our friends and family could see the help we needed? What if we could see the help they needed?

Wouldn't it be great to not hide anymore? Transparency is often praised on social media. However, I think we're only transparent with our feelings but not vulnerable about our needs. It's a whole different ball game to ask for the help we desperately need. Thanks to the highlight reel of social media, we think we know each other. In reality, we only see what others choose to share. In return, we only give the highlight reel of our own lives.

When I was in deep from some bad choices, no one knew that I was struggling so hard. I got to the point where I realized I could no longer hide it. I called a friend who I knew would love me, no matter what I revealed to her. I remember sitting in the parking lot of some restaurant late at night, sobbing my heart out on the phone as I openly shared with her. She didn't shame me. She listened and asked questions. When I asked her for help, she willingly agreed and asked how we could work together to get me out of this hole.

I remember the drive home. I remember breathing deep breaths, feeling freer than I had in a long time. I remember feeling relieved that now someone else would help carry this burden with me. I remember feeling thankful for her and our friendship.

Who can you go to, no matter what, and share what's really going on?

Once we become adults, we are responsible for our choices and for the flow of our lives.

We can't blame others for taking out a large mortgage that now burdens us, or that vacation we took on credit, or those regular "therapy" trips to Target.

Choices, good or bad, have consequences. We can't blame the consequences of our choices on anyone else. We must deal with the consequences. But personal responsibility is hard, isn't it? It's so hard to own, without excuse, that what we did wasn't wise. But when an unwise choice becomes a pattern, then we must look at the why behind those choices.

Even the Apostle Paul knew this struggle: Why do I do the things that I don't want to do And not do the things that I do want to do?!

In the end, only the Creator of you and me can bring the fullness of hope and freedom to every area of our lives. Jesus Christ has redeemed my story. He brought through me that pain to healing. That's His heart for you too—redemption and freedom in Him.

THINK ABOUT IT, WRITE ABOUT IT

Looking back at the motivations you've explored, what do you think are some of the bigger factors for where you are today in your finances? Has He redeemed your story?

Action Day

"Action expresses priorities."

— Gandhi

You made it! Welcome to your last action days. Keep up the momentum!

Step 1: Pick a mini money habit.

Step 2: Go do it. You are stronger than you realize and more capable than you believe.

Step 3: Take the next three days and act on what you chose to do. After you pick your one thing, write below what you will do.

I choose the _____ habit to act on, because

_____

_____

_____

_____

_____

_____

_____

_____

Mini Money Habits

1. Pull your credit report & review it. According to www.ftc.gov, you are entitled to one free credit report every 12 months. Order online from annualcreditreport.com, the only authorized website for free credit reports.

2. Do your will, no matter what your current situation is. You can start with legalzoom.com to get things rolling.

3. Daily check your bank accounts to avoid accruing overdraw fees.

4. Make a list of all of your debts at nerdwallet.com and set up payoff plan.

5. Visit your employer's human resources office and ask for a new W-4 form. Adjust to take as many allowances as possible. This enables you to get more cash in your paycheck, thus giving you more money to put towards your debts or savings.

6. Make a list of your non-monthly expenses, including when and how much. You know, the ones that sneak up on you and karate chop your

bank account? This way you aren't surprised and can plan for them.

7. Pick a utility (car insurance, cell phone plan, etc) & shop around to see if you can get a better deal.

   1. Pro Tip #1 – Use an independent insurance company that will shop all around to find the best deal for your situation.

   2. Pro Tip #2 – Cell phones and related technology has *much improved* over the years. So ignore the popular marketing out there and find the best deal for YOU. Highly recommend non-contract bills.

8. Call the credit card companies to work a deal with them on your interest rate. If your monthly payment is hard to make at this point, ask them to lower it for a set amount of time.

9. Check with your employer about retirement matching contributions. If they do a match, you begin taking that from your paycheck if you aren't already. It's free money, folks, towards your future.

10. If you are on social media, join groups and follow people who inspire action & smart money

habits. Be sure to unfollow those accounts that trigger impulsive spending habits.

11. For the next seven days, track everything you spend. Where is your money going? Why is it going there? Could you do without spending here or there for a month?

12. Research the free budget options available to you. Consider whether you want to use an app, a website, a spreadsheet, or pen and paper. Look into these options and pick one you will commit to using for the next three months. It's not about doing it perfectly, but rather giving it a try. If you like it, then stick with it. If you don't, then try a different method.

13. If you do not have an emergency savings account, then make a plan to save up $500 (single household) or $1000 (family home) as fast as possible.

14. Education in our personal finances should be ongoing. Find a personal finance class in your area to take. This should be repeated every 3-5 years to keep updated on financial strategies as your own life evolves with time.

15. Make a plan for unexpected cash that may come your way this year through birthdays, bonus, side gig, tax return, etc. Decide ahead of time how you need to use that money the best way possible.

16. Check out a book from your local library (it is free) that discusses how wealthy people utilize their money. This contributes to breaking down our misconceptions about what it means to be wealthy.

17. Stop using negative phrases about your money. Cut them out completely, even if they accurately portray your situation. Every time you catch yourself about to say that phrase, replace it with a positive statement. For example, replace "there's never enough money to cover the bills" with "I will find a way to increase my income and reduce my bills."

18. Cut up all of the credit cards that are from department stores. These only entice extra spending in your discretionary categories and they don't save you much money in the end.

19. If you not investing any money, then try using the ACORN app which allows you to invest

your spare change. Investing is simpler than many people believe. Starting small helps break it down into bite-sized pieces.

20. Install the HONEY browser extension on your computer. This nifty app takes action when you are on the checkout page of any online store. It'll scan the web for best deals and promo codes so that you're assured you're getting the best possible deal.

References List

1. Week 1 Day 2 – https://goop.com/wellness/mindfulness/the-scary-power-of-negative-words/

2. Week 3 Day 3 – https://www.mint.com/

3. Week 4 Day 1 – https://www.debtconsolidation.com/debt-throughout-history/

4. Week 4 Day 3 – https://www.thestreet.com/personal-finance/real-estate/least-expensive-us-cities-for-retirees-14956443

5. Week 4 Day 3 – https://www.rewire.org/our-future/millennials-delaying-milestones/

6. Week 4 Day 3 – https://thehill.com/opinion/education/419935-yes-student-loans-really-are-making-millennials-go-broke

7. Week 4 Day 3 – http://luke1428.com/the-most-important-reason-you-do-not-worry-about-tomorrow/

8. Week 7 Day 2 – https://www.goal-cast.com/2019/06/19/brene-brown-quotes/

Share Your Review

Enjoy this book? You can make a big difference.

Reviews are the most powerful tool in my arsenal when it comes to getting attention for this book. Much as I'd like to, I don't have the financial muscle of a big publishing firm. I can't take out full-page ads in the newspaper or post billboards on the highway.

(Not yet, anyway).

But I do have something much more powerful and effective than that, and it's something that those publishers would kill to get their hands on.

A committed and loyal bunch of readers.

Honest reviews of this book help bring it to the attention of other readers.

If you've enjoyed this book and it's helped your life, I would be very grateful if you could spend just five minutes leaving a review on the book's Amazon page. You can jump right to the page by clicking here.

A Note from the Author

Thank you for reading Unlock Your Why! I hope that you enjoyed this book and are excited to share it with your family, friends, and co-workers.

Want to know when I release new books or do you need ongoing inspiration on your financial journey?

Here are some ways to stay connected with me:

Join my email list at www.heatherburgette.com

Follow me on Instagram

Like me on Facebook

And if you have a moment, please review Unlock Your Why online. Help other readers and tell them why you enjoyed reading. You can leave a review here on Amazon. Thank you again, dear reader, and I hope we meet again between the pages of another book.

~Heather

Made in the USA
Lexington, KY
09 November 2019

56600225R00087